W9-ASG-920

Ask the
Fruitcake
Lady

ALSO BY MARIE RUDISILL

The Southern Haunting of Truman Capote

Fruitcake

Sook's Cookbook

Truman Capote

Everything You Would Already Know If You Had Any Sense

Ask the Fruitcake Lady

MARIE RUDISILL

HYPERION

New York

Copyright © 2006 Marie Rudisill

All rights reserved. No part of this book may be used or
reproduced in any manner whatsoever without the written
permission of the Publisher. Printed in the United States
of America. For information address Hyperion,
77 West 66th Street, New York, New York 10023-6298.

LIBRARY OF CONGRESS CATALOGING-IN-PUBLICATION DATA

Rudisill, Marie.
    Ask the fruitcake lady: everything you would already
know if you had any sense/Marie Rudisill.
        p. cm.
    ISBN 1-4013-0317-X
    1. Conduct of life--Miscellanea--Humor. I. Title.
BJ1581.2.R84 2006
818'.60208--dc22

                                    2006043664

Hyperion books are available for special promotions and
premiums. For details contact Michael Rentas, Assistant
Director, Inventory Operations, Hyperion, 77 West 66th
Street, 12th floor, New York, New York 10023, or
call 212-456-0133.

Book design by Richard Oriolo

FIRST EDITION

10 9 8 7 6 5 4 3 2 1

I dedicate this book to my son,

James Rudisill

Contents

Acknowledgments

I've always loved watching *The Tonight Show*. But then, several years ago, I noticed Jay Leno kept talking trash about fruitcake in his opening monologue. He said it was the worst food on the planet, suitable only for building retaining walls. That burned me up, because I knew that he had never actually tasted a good fruitcake. So I wrote him a letter telling him he was uninformed, ignorant, and basically unwelcome, and that if he wanted to taste a real fruitcake he should try some of mine. Of course, he fell in love with me after that. A lot of men are suckers for a strong woman who will put them in their place. A few weeks later, Steve Ridgeway, a *Tonight Show* producer, invited me to appear on the show. Steve was brilliant. He flew me out there first class. He put me up in a nice hotel. And he turned me into a TV star. Steve knew just how to bring out the best in me, and make my appearances such a hit. He and Jay have always treated me so well and made me feel so special. And for that I'll always be loyal to them. Jay continues to flirt with me shamelessly whenever we talk. But I can accept it, because he's so cute. I tell you, if he were a little bit younger, he might even have a chance with me.

Thanks also to my friend Stephen P. Williams. You are a wonderful writer, and you've helped me so much.

Ask the
Fruitcake
Lady

1

The Fruitcake
Lady Answers Your
Questions about
Children

I had an ideal childhood, but I was not the perfect child. I was a real roughneck. I liked doing things that were very dangerous. After my parents died, I was raised by my Aunt Jenny at her big old house in Monroeville, Alabama. There were a bunch of us kids there, including my young nephew, Truman Capote. While Jenny wasn't good at showing love, we knew she cared about us. She never prohibited us from doing things. We lived near the woods, so of course I always wanted to go out there and walk around gathering things, like wild strawberries. But there were a lot of snakes out there. I hate snakes, so I'd put a leash on a pig and he'd walk in front of me and squeal, and that would run the snakes away. That's the kind of thing a kid needs to do.

There are just so many things a parent could tell a child not to do, so many that you couldn't possibly get around to all of them, so you might as well back off. When you let kids do things on their own, then they are better able to cope with life. That's all there is to it.

Q: When I ask my daughter if she's finished her home-work, she just says, "Whatever." It burns me up. What can I do?

A: Nothing. That's their favorite expression. It means they haven't done it, but they will do it. Let 'em go. They're saying "whatever," not "never."

Q: Yesterday my dad told me to do my chores. I said, "No." He said, "What?" I said, "You heard me." Then he swatted me on the butt so hard I could feel the sting all the way through my jeans. Is that the child abuse they were teaching us about at school?

A: Well, aren't you a daisy.

I mean, you felt a sting? Through your jeans? That's not child abuse. That's not even tough love. He could have taken a damned belt to your behind. He could have knocked you right down on it. He could have beat you up right there for talking back to him. But he didn't. He gave you a swat. So listen up: Do your chores! Stop being ridiculous! Lord!

Q: I've got four kids under the age of ten. I like to read the paper when I take them to the playground, they insist that I play with them. What are my rights?

A: You have the right not to take them to the park, you idiot. But if you take them to the park, you should play with them in the park. You're not going there for your pleasure. So why not follow through on it, you selfish bastard?

Q: My friend dopes his daughter up on Starbucks coffee before her field hockey games to make her more competitive. Is this a good idea?

A: **That's absolutely wrong.** He's trying to live through her, and he should get a life of his own. Doping up his own daughter—it's criminal, really. That is the sorriest story I ever heard. And you call him your friend?

Q: The five-year-old boy next door is taking a little too much interest in my five-year-old girl. What should I do?

A: Well, forget the boy. You can't do anything about them. You've got to tell your girl the facts: Boys should not touch girls. And if they try to do that, she should run right home. You tell her never to show a boy anything, even if he promises to show her his thing too. 'Cause he probably won't. And if he did, it wouldn't be that interesting, from what I've seen.

Q: My porky eleven-year-old son looks right at home in his pigsty of a room. When I told him to quit eating fries, he just stuffed one in his mouth and said French people never get fat. What can I do?

A: Well, who gave him the French fries in the first place? The real problem is that if you say no, he just gets upset, and then you go and serve him every damn thing he wants. No wonder he's so unattractive. You're the parent. Just tell him not to eat too much. Let him get upset and jump up and down—the exercise would do him good. I would not give him extra money for French fries. I would not give him money for burgers after school. I mean, Lord, look at your own self. You're probably the biggest hog in that house. How's he going to learn anything from you? How many French fries did you eat today?

Q: I'm twelve, and my parents give me everything I want. I've got the cell phone, the nice jeans, the sunglasses, the Chihuahua with a fake fur coat. How can I get them to stop spoiling me?

A: You must be an exceptional child, because most children would never even think about being spoiled. They'd just ask for more. But you've just got to let your parents be parents, even if they do a terrible job. You can't tell them what to do. You've got to live with being spoiled. Just don't make the same mistakes with your *dog*.

Q: Should children be seen and not heard?

A: Absolutely. They're boring. They shouldn't talk until their first year of college.

Q: My son wants to know if I ever smoked reefer. Well, I did, and sometimes still do. What should I say?

A: Good God, what are you—a drug addict? Smoking marijuana is about the worst thing a person could do. But you've got to tell your child the truth. I don't believe in all these parents sneaking around and doing things they don't want their children to know about. I mean, there are some things— intimate things, like dressing up all fancy and rolling around in the bedroom—that you should keep to yourself, but other than that you should tell them the truth. And warn them about the dangers. And maybe check into rehab yourself.

Q: My folks want me to clean my room. Isn't that what the maid is for?

A: **Well, aren't you some-thing.** The only maid you need is that somebody *made* you clean your room. If you were my child, I'd tell you to get your ass in there and get that room clean. And then you get in there and clean the maid's room too! What'll happen when you leave home and get married? Who is going to clean your room then? I mean, Lord! You might just end up an old maid yourself.

Q: Are children weird, or is it just my imagination?

A: God, are you joking? Jesus Christ, are they strange. Oh, Lord, they've got animal in them. They've got human in them. They are a mixture of everything God ever made. It's like a cocktail. A bad one. I don't ever want another.

Q: My kids refuse to go to sleep at their bedtime, especially when my wife is out of town. What can I do?

A: There's no way that you can force a child to go to sleep. They're going to play with pillows, tear them up, and get feathers all over the damn place. It's just part of their lives. With young kids you could try reading them a story, or offering a bribe, but with teenagers you're just wasting your time. Tell them to go to bed and then go downstairs and have a cup of tea and put them out of your mind. And what's your wife doing out of town anyway?

Q: My kids rebel when I try to impose my marine training methods on the household—it's rare I can bounce a quarter off their beds. How much leeway should I give them?

A: I don't try to stop children too much. I think children should express themselves. You warp a child when you don't allow them to do anything that's brazen. And it's not too good for you, either; fighting them, getting rough with them. I mean, I know sometimes you wonder why God brought this on you and all that, and you just get to feeling like you could kill them, but the law says you can't.

Q: When I try to wake up my son for school, he pretends he's wounded and can't move. What do I do?

A: Oh, God. That is a problem. You've got to take measures there and show him what it might be like to really get wounded. I'd just jerk his covers off and say, "Get the hell out of bed, and I mean get up now." Just scream and cuss at him. In utter anger he'll get out of the bed. He'll sit down at the breakfast table and sulk. But you don't give a damn about whether he eats his cereal or not. Then when the school bus comes, you start yelling till he gets his ass up out of the chair and onto the bus. School's important. Breakfast isn't.

Q: My fourteen-year-old daughter hangs out with a girl who talks back, lives on junk food, and never does her homework. I can't stand her values, but my daughter thinks she's cool. What can I do?

A: You're the parent, aren't you? You tell her, look, you're not going to be friends with that girl; that's all there is to it, and if you do see her, there are going to be serious consequences. If she resists, you must really pound her down by cutting off every advantage that she has. No phone, no allowance, no candy, no TV. You just sew her up. Oh, she'll cry and carry on and all that. But in cases like this, you've got to be firm. Absolutely. In the end, she'll respect you for it. Children are strange in this way.

2

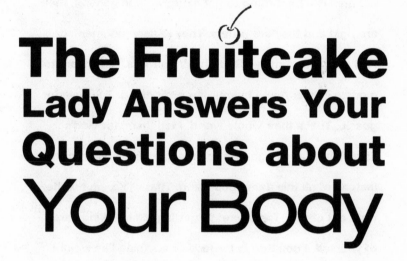

The Fruitcake
Lady Answers Your
Questions about
Your Body

Now, my body, it's getting old, but I'm still strong.

Everybody young is mystified by that. They think you just shrivel up and disappear, but you don't. Some old people, however, get real difficult. Like old men. An old man is a hard thing to get along with. In general, they are rigid and they are ornery. They're very judgmental. And then old women—God, they're a mess. They want to meddle in everything in your life. Everything. They live for gossip. That's their whole world. I tell them, for God's sakes, start a rose garden or do something constructive, instead of all this damn gossiping. That will drain the life right out of you. The secret to getting old is taking care of yourself. I don't go in for fads or anything like weight lifting or walking. I just do as I damn please and roll along with life as it comes. That's all you've got to do.

Q: Is youth wasted on the young?

A: Of course not. It's wasted by old people who think they could do it better, if only they had the chance—which they won't.

Q: What is the secret to longevity? (Not that at age ninety-five, you would know.)

A: Just live a normal life and don't go to extremes. Be moderate. Don't drink, don't smoke. I used to smoke. Oh Lord, it was terrible. And then I just realized all of a sudden that I was killing myself with smoking, and I just stopped before I died. That was ten years ago. I was eighty-five.

Q: Should I pay extra for soft bathroom tissue, or save money on the rough stuff?

A: Your ass won't know the difference.

Q: My wife says I'm lazy for wanting to nap in the afternoon. Do you nap?

A: Your wife is right, poor thing.
Nothing's worse than a lazy man. I never nap, and I'm ninety-five years old. I get into bed each night with my pit bull, Crissy, and we watch Jay Leno. It's part of my job to keep up with the show. Especially when I'm on it. Jay once said to me, "My God, you mean to tell me you get into bed with a pit bull?" I said, "Of course, Jay—and she won't let anybody else come into the room." I think he might have been sad to hear that.

Q: Is it possible to cry when you're underwater?

A: Who the hell cares whether you cry under- water or you don't? I've never heard of anything as foolish as that. Oh Lord, that was a stupid question.

Q: My wife is begging for a boob job. I'm horrified, and told her I'd divorce her if she got one. Am I being too stubborn?

A: **I think you're right. She shouldn't do it.** If you're happy with the way her breasts are, even if they are small or saggy or whatever, she should be happy too. I think all this medical stuff is very dangerous, and eventually they'd have to go back in there and take that stuff out and restuff it. She'd start to feel like a horned sheep on somebody's trophy wall. I wouldn't let her. But you've got to make her feel that you like it the way it is. Let her know that not all men need overinflated balloons to play with.

Q: How do I get my husband to stop adjusting his privates in public?

A: That is the worst habit any man on earth can have. Just clawing at his dick every time he goes out to the mall, putting it over here and moving it over there—I don't know why any woman would put up with that kind of disgusting behavior. I would just tell him, look, you do all the playing you want here at home, but you're not going to fondle yourself out in public like you've got some kind of pet in your pants that you've got to take care of. It's sickening.

Q: Scientists have found a virus that causes obesity. How can I avoid catching it?

A: **What's that virus called— the gut-stuffer virus?** The fat-cheeked-jiggle-butt-give-me-another-donut virus? The I'm-a-piggy-wiggy virus? The I-can't-control-myself-so-I'm-gonna-go-blame-some-little-inno-cent-virus-that-doesn't-know-a-cream-puff-from-a-salad? The only way you can avoid that virus is by keeping your jaws closed.

Q: Why did God give us wrinkles?

A: It's to remind people to act their age. There are way too many people these days that are acting teenile instead of senile.

Q: Statistics show that widowers die younger than men who are married. I don't understand.

A: Just look down at your penis. That's all the explanation you need. Men in general can die from not having sex. That's what they're all about. Still, even though most of these old widowers are rigid, it's not necessarily in the way that a woman needs. These softies wouldn't be a lady's first choice.

Q: My grannie's Victoria's Secret catalogue is just brimming with Post-it Notes, including a hot pink one flagging a sheer teddy-stocking combo. Isn't she too old for lingerie?

A: What difference does it make how old a woman is? Some women wear lingerie well into their sixties and seventies. Some of them still wear string underwear, for God's sake. It's ridiculous, sure, but no more ridiculous than a seventeen-year-old using a piece of string to cover her butt. It just depends on the individual woman, and how she feels about herself. What does it matter? How come you're asking me such a dumb question? Just remember those Post-its when her next birthday rolls around.

Q: Do you think cosmetic surgery is good?

A: I wouldn't recommend it to anybody. I think you should do the best you can to always look good, but remember, there are ugly people who are very interesting, and I think they should remain that way. While, generally, prettier people seem to have an easier time of it, sometimes ugly people have much better character and can do things with their lives that a better-looking person wouldn't bother to do. Beauty can be a real curse. Sometimes a person will depend on her beauty instead of her brains, to her everlasting sorrow. And if that beauty's faked up by some doctor? Well, even a dog could spot that.

Q: My college-age son is averse to bathing. He comes home stinking like a bear and tells me the smell is God's gift—he doesn't want to mess with Mother Nature. What do you think of that?

A: **You ought to knock the living crap out of him.** You are the mother—take charge! He shouldn't be allowed to stink. That's sickening. He should take a shower every day. Maybe two. Plus deodorant and maybe a squirt of cologne. How'd you raise that boy? Good Lord.

Q: Is it okay for a man to get his butt waxed?

A: **If that's what he wants, yes.** I don't see the point of it, but it's not my butt.

3

The Fruitcake
Lady Answers Your
Questions about
Love

There's no way to know in advance if a relationship is going to work. You can go through the wedding happy as all get-out and then find yourself feeling miserable before you unpack your lingerie at the honeymoon suite. My family didn't approve of my first marriage, because my husband was Japanese. This was back in the 1930s. So they found a friendly judge down in Monroeville, Alabama, who got us divorced and kept everything on the Q.T. But I really loved that man. He was so talented and such a sweet, wonderful person. And I would have been a lot happier with him than I was with the man I married after that. I mean, that one just drank so much, it was miserable. A man who drinks excessively, it's not a happy marriage. We loved each other, but we had our times. So you never know how it's going to turn out. I don't think anyone has to get married to be happy. I think you can live alone happily your whole life. You just have to see what life gives you and move forward from there. There's not a damn thing else you can do.

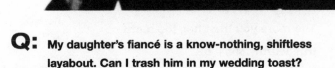

Q: My daughter's fiancé is a know-nothing, shiftless layabout. Can I trash him in my wedding toast?

A: Toast? You've got to stop it long before you blow any of your money on champagne. Don't be nice about it. It's very hard to convince a girl that she's going to ruin her life if she marries a lout. Girls are headstrong that way. They might even be dumb. Most times, you've got to let them figure things out on their own. But this could be a tragedy. Don't let her do it. It would be like throwing your daughter in the trash.

Q: My wife works, and wants to have her own bank account, separate from our joint account. I think that's ridiculous. She said to ask you.

A: When did you get appointed chairman of the Federal Home Reserve? Hell, when I was married, I worked all the time and I handled my own damn money. If she's got sense enough to earn it, she's got sense enough to know how to spend it. Admit it—you're just afraid of losing control of the woman, aren't you? I'll tell you a secret: The more you trust her, the more trustworthy she'll be.

Q: My wedding ring gives me a rash. Is it OK to go without it? My wife's afraid I'll start sniffing around.

A: No, you don't have to wear your ring. Sure, it's a sign to the world that you're married, but it's not a security system a wife can depend on. When a man's eye starts to wander while he's sitting in some nasty bar, he's just going to slip the ring into his change pocket anyway. What the hell. Take the ring off. It's not gonna make a damn bit of difference to your marriage, as long as it's not your wife that's causing the allergy. But tell me, how would you feel if she quit wearing hers?

Q: I want to break up with my girlfriend, but I'm thinking of waiting until after Christmas, because she always gives good presents. Is this OK?

A: Oh, how selfish can you be? Is it because you found another girl? If so, break up with the first one and hope for the best with the second one. It'd serve you right to wake up one morning with a lump of coal on your pillow, you fool.

Q: I just got out of college. I'm looking for a good man, the kind that changes diapers, cooks casseroles, gives me a neck rub, and still brings home good bacon. Where can I find him?

A: In fantasyland, which is obviously where you live. That's so ridiculous. No man on earth is going to do all that. And why would you want it? That would be so boring. You must be a lazy bitch. You have to be, to want a man like that.

Q: The first anniversary, you're supposed to give a gift made out of paper, but I can't think of anything. How can I let my wife know I cherish her?

A: Well, that's easy. Paper money. Lots of it.

Q: I like this guy, and we talk and everything, but he's never asked me out. My friend says I should ask him instead. What do you think?

A: If he hasn't asked you, why would you want to embarrass yourself by being foolish enough to ask him? Either he doesn't want you, or he's not man enough. Either way, you wouldn't want that date. A lady should never do the asking.

Q: My girlfriend loves the beach, but I get all blotchy in the sun. I like the mountains, but she's scared of heights. What should we do?

A: Split up.

Q: Is it as easy for a woman to marry rich as it is to marry poor?

A: No. That's a ridiculous idea. You can give it a try, but it's not going to happen except by accident. I mean, you can't control that. Rich people only associate with other rich people—to meet them, you've got to be flying first-class yourself. Most of these men are already married anyway, to rich women. In fact, that's probably how most of 'em got rich in the first place.

Q: 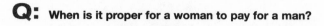 When is it proper for a woman to pay for a man?

A: Any man that would let a woman pay for a date is not worth paying for.

Q: What do you think of sex before marriage?

A: **It's a good idea to have sex before you get married to a fellow.** Most of the time, to be truthful, people just aren't compatible in that way. And that's a very important part of a marriage. So go at it. Just don't expect too much.

Q: My dog goes crazy whenever the bitch across the street goes into heat. If I let him out and that dog gets pregnant, am I obligated to contribute to the upkeep of those puppies?

A: **You shouldn't let your dog out in the first place, you bastard.** But yes, you'd be liable for puppy support. And I hope it's a big litter.

Q: What do you call a man who stays home cleaning the house and watching the kids while his wife goes out and works?

A: **A sucker.**

Q: Should I tell my best friend that his girl is cheating on him?

A: **Oh Lord, I hate people that cheat.** I'd tell him. Absolutely. You're in a bad spot, though. He's going to get mad and call you a liar. I mean, she's a bum and a tramp, but he's still going to love her. That's how men are. I do not understand it. And when he calls you a liar, just say, "OK, go find out for yourself, you stupid bastard." Your friendship will work itself out over time.

4

The Fruitcake Lady Answers Your Questions about Home

Before my parents died, my father raised racehorses, and we had a nice house and barns. It was lovely. Then I moved into the big house with my Aunt Jenny, which had beautiful gardens, and a fence in the backyard made out of animal bones she'd collected from a pet cemetery. I've always loved having a nice home. When I lived in Charlotte, my husband and I had a beautiful old three-story place, with herb gardens and nice furnishings. I was in the antique business, and had a collection of Baccarat paperweights. We had beautiful gardens; we had roses, lots of them. And four varieties of mint that would smell so wonderful when you put it in your iced tea. You could walk in my garden and get whatever you wanted for dinner. I don't know why young people don't have herb gardens anymore. They're too busy shopping for vegetables at the store.

Q: My wife wants to put a bidet in our new bathroom. I find that kind of scary. I'd rather put in a nice porcelain urinal. What do you think?

A: A bidet is a very civilized thing to have, a rather nice thing to do. A urinal would be uncivilized. It belongs in a bar, which is where you'll be spending your lonely evenings if you don't get more considerate of your wife.

Q: My fiancée has yellow teeth. Am I right to suspect that if she can't take care of her own mouth now, she won't keep a good house after we're married?

A: I don't see what damn difference it would make to you. If you can snuggle up to yellow teeth, you can live in a filthy house. I wouldn't even worry about housekeeping till I took care of that dental problem. What are you, desperate? It would make me sick to look at someone with yellow teeth all day long, let alone kiss them. Get her some bleach. And an industrial toothbrush.

Lord. Some people are so stupid, I can't believe it.

Q: My ten-year-old says I'm being a freak for not letting her paint her room black. What do you think?

A: I think you're being a freak for asking me this crazy question. Of course she can't paint her room black. It is a very depressing color. This is one of those times you've just got to step in. You're the parent. Don't let your children control you. God gave you those children to oversee, and if you let them be overbearing, you're going to have nothing but tragedy. You'll die young, and she'll get to wear black to your funeral.

Q: I'm a bit of a perfectionist, and I want my lawn to reflect that. But I have a conundrum: How can I install a sign saying "Keep off the grass" without walking on the lawn myself?

A: Well, that's an impossible task, even for a perfectionist. But it's a crazy idea anyway. I mean, that is just plain downright stupid. It's not going to kill the lawn to walk on it. A lawn is supposed to be a beautiful place. People put chairs out there. They have barbecues out there. What's the matter with you, man? I've got a beautiful lawn in my backyard, but we eat out there on picnic tables. We enjoy it. Are you going to invite your friends over to look at the grass?

Q: My wife's mother lives next door to us, and she doesn't knock before entering our house. My wife is afraid to say anything to her. Should I?

A: **Well, you're an idiot for living next door to your mother-in-law in the first place.** That's for sure. But I appreciate your problem. Very rarely does a person, man or woman, get along with his mother-in-law. They are just too interfering. That's their whole reason for living. So you've just got to be straight with her. Say, "Listen up, you better start knocking on my door before you come in, or else you can just go to hell, you understand?" You can get real rough with her. What do you care? If your wife starts crying, just let her cry. In the long run she'll respect you for it, because even if she doesn't say so, I can't imagine that your wife's too happy with the situation either.

Q: I hate my job, but I love the money, because it pays for my great house. What should I do?

A: A fool and his money are soon parted. I'm sure you've heard that. Can't you get another job? Do the thing that makes you happy. Keep the house; get more money. It's never too late to make a career change. Look at me. I didn't start on *Jay Leno* till I was ninety.

Q: I'm going to put a fence up around my front yard, for privacy. Should I put the good side of the fence facing in, where I can see it, and leave the bad side facing out for the neighbors, or vice versa?

A: **Your neighbor isn't required to look at the ugly side of your fence, you fool.** It's always been done that the good side faces out, and nothing in the world has changed about that. But I see where you might have gotten the idea, since you seem to be showing me your ugly side right now.

Q: My fiancée likes grits with cheese. I like them with butter. Are we compatible?

A: Isn't that silly—it's just grits. It doesn't matter how you like them. Just cook the grits and put 'em on the table. If she wants cheese, let her have cheese. And plop some butter on your own plate. I mean, my God, have we gotten to the stage where we supervise each other's eating? Has it come to that? What you gonna do, put grits in the prenup?

Q: I been told that it's proper to serve bottled water in crystal glasses, rather than the tumblers I use for tap water. Is that correct?

A: The only difference between bottled water and tap water is that bottled water makes you feel like a big shot, even if you aren't.

Q: My neighbors said I could use their pool whenever I wanted. But when they found me doing laps butt naked, they got mad and kicked me out. What's up with that?

A: Well, first I'd wonder if you know what you really look like. And second, I'd wonder how well you know your friends. Of course you have a right to go skinny-dipping, but maybe you should do it in your own water. Many people do not like to see somebody naked, because a naked person is not a pretty person. I don't give a damn who you are.

Q: I say it's sexist for my wife to insist that I leave the seat down when I'm finished peeing. What do you think?

A: **If you'd learn to pee straight, you might have a case to make.** But a man, he'll pull it out and start peeing all over the seat, all around the inside of the lid, on the floor, and anywhere except in the bowl. Just like a dog. Evidently there's something wrong with the design of a man, because they can't aim. Although knowing men, I'm sure they would blame it on the toilet.

5

The Fruitcake Lady Answers Your Questions about Behavior

As a Southerner, I was raised to behave well. I absolutely think good manners are important in a person's life. I see children these days growing up with no manners, and I can't stand a child like that. I mean, they come to the table and eat like pigs. When I was a child, we never raised a fork, not a bite of food entered our mouths, until my Aunt Jenny raised hers first. That was understood. I believe that is a thing of beauty, to be a well-mannered child. But the damn parents, they don't train them anymore. They're working all the time to pay for school and cars and refrigerators. Their jobs always come first. It's a tragedy. Where have the manners gone?

Q: Is truthfulness next to godliness?

A: Yes, the Bible tells you so. But everyone has lied, at some point, including me. Sometimes a lie is justi-fied, such as if someone's dying of a terminal ill-ness and you don't want to tell them. Or if your blind date is just so ugly it would break her heart to tell her the truth about why you aren't going to ask her out again. The truth is, you don't want to have ugly children.

Q: I know it's polite to give up your seat for a pregnant woman. But just how pregnant does she have to be?

A: What you going to do— walk up to her and say, "Hey, when did he do that to you?" Let's just say it's a nice gesture to give your seat up for a pregnant woman, no matter how big they are. But we all know that not too many men are going to do that.

Q: Are my kids right that I'm setting a bad example by sneaking snacks and drinks into the movie theater to save money?

A: **That's ridiculous.** You aren't doing anything wrong. You're just trying to be economical, because the prices they charge are just exorbitant. Tell the kids that if they don't like it, they don't have to eat it. And if they don't like hearing that, they don't need to go to the movies in the first place.

Q: I came across my boss's online résumé and noticed he told a few big whoppers about his history. Should I rat him out to his boss, or just blackmail him?

A: Neither. What business is it of yours? I mean, you're a bastard for even thinking about that. It won't get you ahead. It will get you in the behind, a good kick in the behind, eventually. The truth always comes out, you know, and yours might actually be worse than his. This is an ugly thing you're proposing.

Q: What's better for men—boxers or briefs?

A: Boxers. They hide more. And that's a good thing.

Q: I just read that some plastic surgeons now work on dogs. Should I get my poodle improved?

A: Oh Lord, isn't that sick. Why torture a dog with something like that? I mean, a dog is just a dog, so let him be a dog. You thought he was good-looking when you got him, right? What's different now? I don't know why people want to make animals suffer.

Q: I go to a fancy gym. The other guys often leave their dirty clothes all over the bench while they take a shower. Can I shove their sweaty stuff to the floor to make room for my own butt?

A: You don't have to shove them to the floor, fool. Just take your hand or, if you're too precious, use a paper towel, and push them to the side to make a little room. I hope your butt's not that big that you would have to have the whole bench.

Q: Are wireless cell phone headsets the work of the devil?

A: Who else would design something crazy like that? People don't need a cell phone in the first place, and to see them walking around yakking into the air with one of these wireless things like they're a bunch of lunatics on the sidewalk—well, that's ridiculous. What the hell are they talking on the phone about anyway— where to find a good oncologist? I think those headsets cause brain cancer.

Q: Should grown men wear nut-huggers at the beach?

A: Nope. No sir. Not at all.

Those swimsuits are intended only for Olympians. They expose too much. And those are not pretty objects to look at. It's kind of like taking your engine out of the car and mounting it on the hood.

Q: I'm a vegan, because I can't stand the thought of killing things. I keep getting invited to dinner parties where they serve pork chops. What can I do?

A: Call ahead to tell them you're a weirdo. I mean, you've got a problem.

Q: When we travel, my boss always flies first-class, and puts me back in coach. What do you think?

A: That's demeaning. I think a boss like that, he doesn't really care about you. I'd get me another job.

Q: Studies show that plants thrive when people talk to them. Do you talk to your plants?

A: Oh, come on. What would I do, say, "Hello, Celery, how are you? Do you want me to dice you up?" You'd be better off talking to God.

Q: The guy in the cubicle next to me always eats Indian food at lunch, then spends the whole afternoon farting. When I complained, he accused me of being too uptight. What can I do about it?

A: **I'd build a higher partition, I think.** That's about the only thing you can do. That or start smoking, and blowing it his way. Maybe snack on stinky cheese. Or take up farting yourself.

6

The Fruitcake
Lady Answers Your
Questions about
Sex

Sex is important at any age. I'm ninety-five, and I openly admit that since my husband died, I have missed having sex. I get some interest, but none that I'm interested in. An eighty-four-year-old man wrote me a letter saying I was his ideal woman, and asking if I would live with him. I said, if you think I'm going to nurse some damn eighty-four-year-old man, you're crazy. I mean, if he was twenty-four, maybe. But why would I want to sleep with a dirty old man? God. He couldn't get it up if he had to. Even Viagra wouldn't work. For all their talk, I don't really think men are as promiscuous as women. They're too scared.

Q: My wife keeps saying she wants "foreplay." What the heck is she talking about?

A: You are a fool. I'm amazed that you even have a wife. She wants you to fondle her, stupid. She wants you to kiss her, maybe love her breasts all over. Now that's foreplay. You see, a woman doesn't really want sex in the beginning. She needs to be coaxed, and just looking at you dangling in all your glory isn't going to do the trick. If you want a woman that will wiggle, and I know you do, then foreplay is the only thing that will motivate her. Hey, you might even find that you enjoy it yourself.

Q: Why do women take longer to have an orgasm? I sometimes miss my TV shows waiting for my girlfriend to finish.

A: Well Lordy, with someone like you, I'm surprised she ever gets started in the first place. Aren't you a selfish one. The woman is physically different from the man, thank God. A man can stick it in there and have an orgasm in a second, and then give his love to the TV. But it takes a woman a while to really enjoy the experience. She's got a canal down there, and you've got to enter it the right way, and that takes time. I can't explain it to you. It just does.

Q: Does size matter?

A: If a man is built too large, it might hurt the woman.

There's no question about it. It hurts. But then again, a man that's built too short and stubby, he's not gonna be a good bed partner either. A woman likes a man that has a penis that is not too big, not too small, a bit long and a bit thin so it fits in there just right. But look, what are you going to do—get a new penis at the penis store? You've got to work with what you've got.

Q: Should I buy my wife sex toys for Christmas?

A: No. That's an abuse of the body. You'll pay for it later on, because it will damage her organs. She'll use it so much she'll ruin her body. She'll get cancer or bleed. I don't believe in that at all.

Q: I hate condoms. What do you suggest?

A: I suggest you don't have sex.

Q: What does it mean that my girlfriend hums and twitters like a deranged songbird when we have sex?

A: Well, that's an odd one. I've never heard of that. But it sounds good to me. It must mean that you're one of the world's greatest lovers, and you must have given her a super thrill. Or else you're making it up.

Q: What's the difference between a stud and a slut?

A: Well, the stud is a much-admired creature. Everybody thinks he's got a big penis, and not some little old wormy-looking thing. A slut is a much-hated creature—except when a stud is looking for some action—whom all the women and men treat badly. They say she'll spread her legs for anybody. But in truth, without studs, sluts wouldn't exist.

Q: I'm getting married next week, and I have to confess that I hate looking at my fiancé's penis. I've seen others that I like a lot more. Is there anything I can do about that?

A: Dear Lord, I don't know what to tell you. That's a tragedy. The best thing you can do is just not marry him, because it is only going to build up until you're at the point where you absolutely hate him. Why did you just now get around to looking at his penis?

Q: Which came first, the chicken or the egg?

A: Sex.

Q: A girl at work smiles at me as though she wants a little interoffice male. In fact, I'd like to make love with her on top of the copy machine and send copies to all my friends. Is office sex OK?

A: Oh, for God's sakes, this is one of the most disgusting questions I've ever been asked. That's lust, not love. If you're in love with anything, it's your own damn self. What could make you think anyone wants to look at your stuff on some photocopy? And to do it in the office? That's a place of business, not a place of sex. Oh, Lord. My God. Just be sure to clean the machine when you're done.

Q: If there were a female orgasm pill, would a woman ever choose a man?

A: They'd take the pill every time.

Q: What happens to a man who doesn't have sex?

A: He withdraws from society. He loses his mind. He begins to masturbate, which is a nasty thing for me to say, but what else are they going to do? I would rather see a man go with a woman any day of the week than go in the bathroom and masturbate.

7

The Fruitcake
Lady Answers Your
Questions about
Faith

The first thing every morning, I go into my living room and sit in my chair and pray to God. My pit bull, Crissy, watches me. I was dragged to church when I was a child, but I came to my faith later, on my own. I think that we all can have a relationship with God, if we seek it. People just lose track. They pile sins on top of sins in their lives. Like money—they let it govern their lives, which is a terrible sin, you know. And then the other things in life—sex and all that—they just make your heart wicked. You know it at the time, but you go ahead and do it. You bring it upon yourself. If you want to be free of sin, just pray sincerely to God to forgive you. He will. I know that God hears me, no matter where I am. I can be out in the yard. I can be in the toilet. He'll get back to me on his own schedule. And not always with exactly what I want to hear.

Q: When I start saying the blessing before dinner, my kids shake their heads and say food comes from the grocery store, not God. Am I right to insist?

A: Yes, but keep it short. Just thank God for the food and say amen. I've gone to people's homes for dinner and when they start praying, Lordy, it seems like they're never going to quit. It's like the damn Academy Awards. You don't want that. And next time your kids make that smart remark, ask them where the grocery store came from.

Q: My friend visits a guru from India for group meditation. The guru told him that if enough people meditate together, they can actually bring about world peace. Should I help them out?

A: Well, that's a hell of a thing. But it ain't going to bring about nothing but a lot of hot air. Who's he trying to kid? Oh, good God. Meditate on this: The world is full of crazy people. And you're one of them.

Q: Does God have long shirttails, and if so, what are they made of?

A: **Oh, yes, indeed he does have wonderfully long shirttails.** Just grab on to one and he'll pull you through anything. I would guess they're made of angel's hair, but it don't matter whether it's hand-sewn Egyptian cotton or 100 percent rayon. In fact, that's about the dumbest question I've ever heard.

Q: If the longest journey begins with the first step, why take it?

A: **'Cause the longest journey is the only one that counts.** My God, there are so many times in your life that you've got to take that first step. Otherwise nothing good will ever happen to you. And if you can't step, crawl, you lazy bastard. It's a wonder you can find your way to the bathroom.

Q: I saw a story about a guy who sat in a cave on top of a mountain for years, looking for the truth. Do you think he found it?

A: Sounds like a publicity hound to me. You don't need to go to a mountaintop, or a cave, or even to a cathedral to find the truth. You can pray to God in a fruit cellar if you want. God doesn't care where you pray, or how. You don't even need to get on your knees to do it. The truth is right in front of you, always all around you. I mean, praying in a cave might get you on TV, but it won't necessarily get you into heaven.

Q: Can I give up Lent for Lent?

A: Well, some people give up drinking. Some people give up smoking. Some people, I suppose, would like to give up the whole idea of giving something up. So go right ahead.

Q: I take my kids to church every Sunday, and it bores the hell out of them. Should I fess up that it bores the hell out of me too?

A: I think so, because, basically, unless the minister is a real dynamic personality, going to church is the most boring thing in the world. I was forced to go to the Baptist church when I was young. I used to hate that worse than poison. I don't think you should force religion down children's throats. Forcing them to go to listen to some old man who shouldn't be a minister in the first place, well, that's torture, and the inquisition was supposed to have ended a long time back.

Q: If God is good, why is the world so bad?

A: He's got to show us he's the boss. And it's best not to give him any back talk.

Q: Is it OK to take an extra gulp of the Communion wine?

A: **What are you, an alcoholic?** Of course it's not OK. It's a very religious thing you're doing, with a lot of tradition behind it, and you should abide by the rules. Anyway, that's not fine wine they're serving. You'd be better off buying your own.

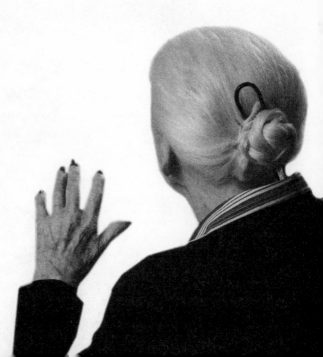

Q: What five outfits will I wear in heaven?

A: Oh, for heaven's sakes.
I don't know. You may not wear anything in heaven,
because you just might go straight to hell.

Q: Is the Communion wafer really Christ's flesh? And if so,
isn't that cannibalism?

A: Good God, what are you asking that for? Of course it's not.
Flesh would probably taste better.